Contact Us:

MyBibleWorkbooks@gmail.com

Projectkingdomcome

Projectkingdomcome

PROJECT KINGDOM COME
ISBN 978-1-961786-13-4

Get The Entire Workbook Series!

SCAN ME

THE BOOK OF GENESIS
BIBLE-BASED WORKBOOK
Take an adventure into the amazing Book of Genesis and test your knowledge as you go!

PROJECT KINGDOM COME

THE BOOKS OF EXODUS & JOSHUA
BIBLE-BASED WORKBOOK
Take an adventure into the amazing Books of Exodus and Joshua and test your knowledge as you go!

PROJECT KINGDOM COME

THE BOOKS OF I & II SAMUEL
BIBLE-BASED WORKBOOK
Take an adventure into the amazing Books of 1st and 2nd Samuel and test your knowledge as you go!

PROJECT KINGDOM COME

THE BOOKS OF I & II KINGS
BIBLE-BASED WORKBOOK
Take an adventure into the amazing Books of 1st and 2nd Kings and test your knowledge as you go!

PROJECT KINGDOM COME

THE BOOKS OF ESTHER & RUTH
BIBLE-BASED WORKBOOK
Take an adventure into the amazing Books of Esther and Ruth and test your knowledge as you go!

PROJECT KINGDOM COME

THE BOOKS OF DANIEL & JOB
BIBLE-BASED WORKBOOK
Take an adventure into the amazing Books of Daniel and Job and test your knowledge as you go!

PROJECT KINGDOM COME

THE BOOK OF MATTHEW
BIBLE-BASED WORKBOOK
Take an adventure into the amazing Book of Matthew and test your knowledge as you go!

PROJECT KINGDOM COME

THE BOOK OF MARK
BIBLE-BASED WORKBOOK
Take an adventure into the amazing Book of Mark and test your knowledge as you go!

PROJECT KINGDOM COME

THE BOOK OF LUKE
BIBLE-BASED WORKBOOK
Take an adventure into the amazing Book of Luke and test your knowledge as you go!

PROJECT KINGDOM COME

THE BOOK OF JOHN
BIBLE-BASED WORKBOOK
Take an adventure into the amazing Book of John and test your knowledge as you go!

PROJECT KINGDOM COME

THE BOOK OF ACTS
BIBLE-BASED WORKBOOK
Take an adventure into the amazing Book of Acts and test your knowledge as you go!

PROJECT KINGDOM COME

THE BOOK OF REVELATION
BIBLE-BASED WORKBOOK
Take an adventure into the amazing Book of Revelation and test your knowledge as you go!

PROJECT KINGDOM COME

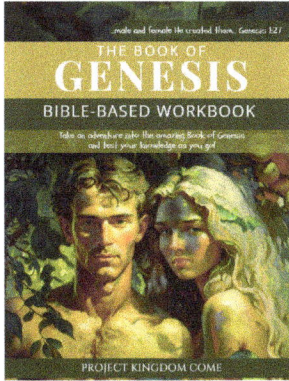

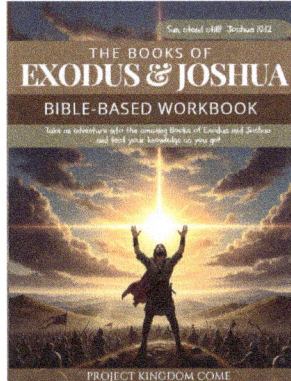

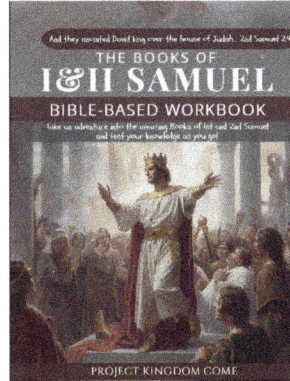

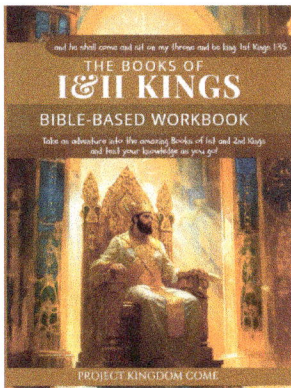

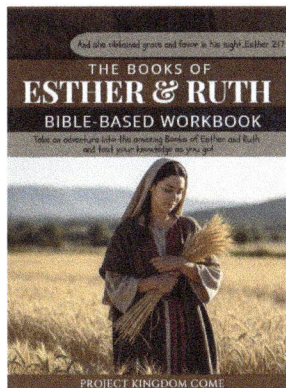

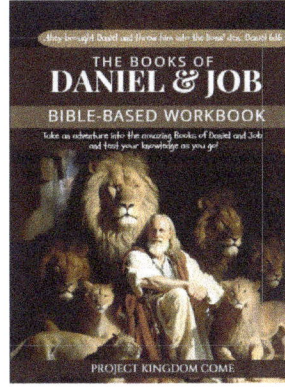

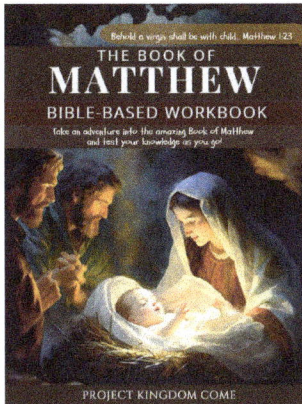

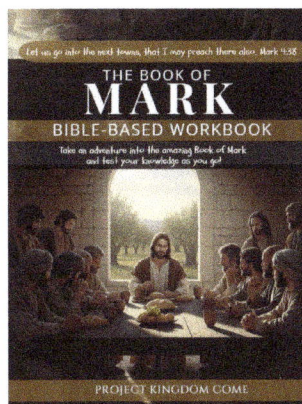

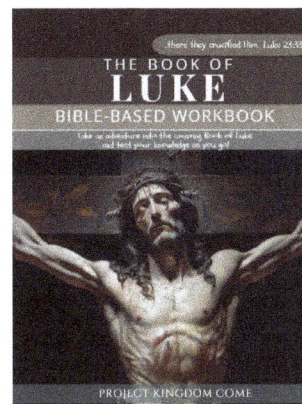

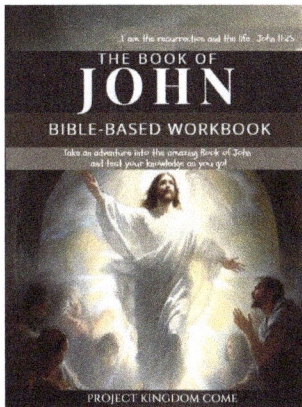

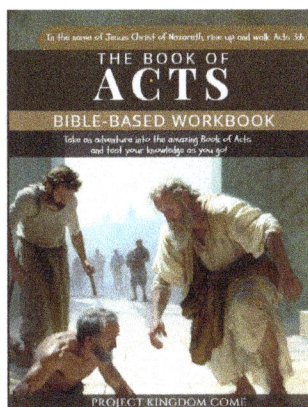

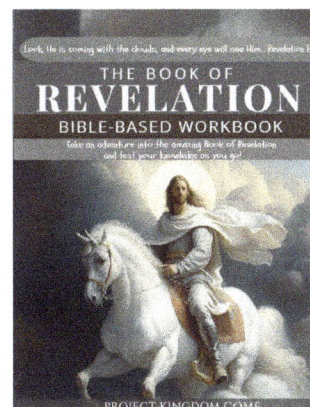

WWW.MYBIBLEWORKBOOKS.COM

PROJECT KINGDOM COME
Spread the Word

This workbook belongs to:

_____

_____

_____

Leave your mark!

HOW TO USE THIS WORKBOOK

This workbook is designed to help young people explore the treasures in God's Word while having fun, growing in faith, and learning how to search the Scriptures for life's answers.

Here is what you will find inside:

Multiple Choice Questions
Each question comes directly from Scripture and includes a reference verse to help with locating the answer in the Bible. If possible, use a physical Bible to search for the answers.

Weekly Segments
Questions are grouped in weekly categories that could also be completed in a shorter or longer time frame.

Weekly Memory Verses
At the start of every week is a Bible verse to memorize. Each day of that week will repeat that memory verse with a chance to test memorization at the end of the week.

Certificate of Completion
At the end of the workbook, please find a Certificate of Achievement, ready for the child's name and parent or teacher's signature. Celebrate the accomplishment of studying an entire book in the Bible!

Answer Key
The workbook contains an answer key to serve as a support tool for parents or teachers reviewing the responses.

Recommendation for Parents and/or Teachers: Review the responses with your child or student and discuss lessons learned or interesting insights, to improve the child's retention and enrichment in the knowledge of God's word.

You can do all things through Christ who gives you strength!
Philippians 4:13

SAMPLE QUESTION...

HOW TO USE THIS WORKBOOK

> Reading the reference verse will always lead you to the correct answer!

In the beginning, God created: (Genesis 1:1)

A The Heavens and the Earth
B. Heaven and Earth
C. Heaven only
D. Earth only

> The number that comes after the book is the 'Chapter'

> This is the name of a book in the Bible

Joshua 1:8

> The number after the chapter is the 'Verse'

NOW TEST YOURSELF! FIND JOSHUA CHAPTER 1 VERSE 8 IN YOUR BIBLE!

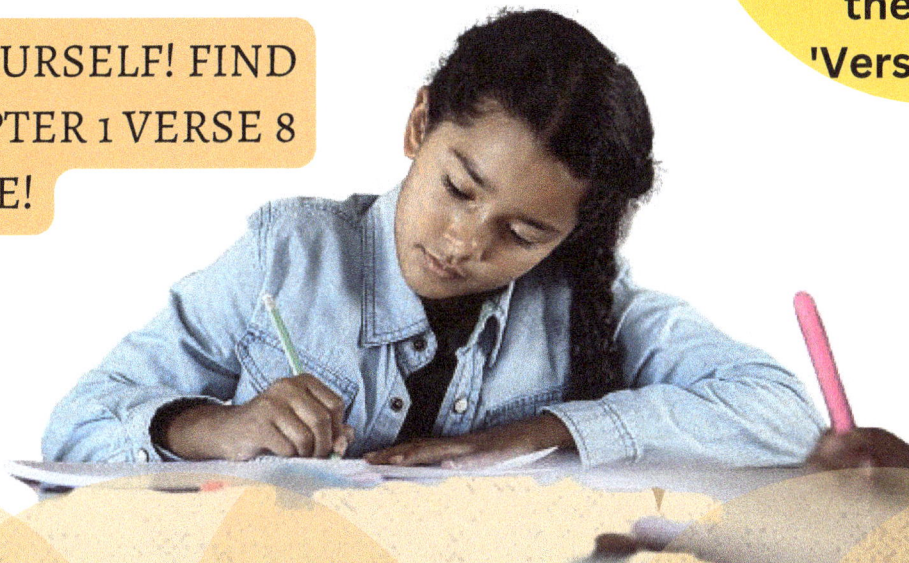

INTRODUCTION: THE BOOK OF EXODUS

The God Who Delivers

The Book of Exodus is the amazing story of how **God delivered His people** from slavery in Egypt and led them into freedom. The word Exodus means "**a going out,**" and it shows us that no matter how hard life gets, **God always makes a way!**

In this book, you will meet **Moses,** the man God chose to lead the Israelites. You will see how God performed **many miracles,** how **He split the Red Sea**, gave the **Ten Commandments**, and showed His people how to live in freedom and to trust Him.

As you study Exodus, remember:
- **God hears our cries and answers**
- **God is powerful and full of glory**
- **God gives us His law to help us live His way**
- **God leads, protects, and provides every step of the journey**

Even when the Israelites were afraid or didn't understand, **God stayed with them**. And He is with you too — leading, guiding, and calling you to trust Him with all your heart.

"The Lord will fight for you; you need only to be still." - Exodus 14:14

WEEK 1

1. **Why did the Egyptians become afraid of the Israelites? (Exodus 1: 8-12)**

   A. The Israelites were preparing to fight Egypt
   B. The Israelites were growing in number and strength
   C. The Israelites looked like giants
   D. The Israelites wanted to leave Egypt

2. **Who were Shiphrah and Puah, and what did Pharaoh tell them to do? (Exodus 1: 15-17)**

   A. Egyptian doctors told to treat Hebrew slaves
   B. Midwives told to kill all newborn Hebrew boys
   C. Palace servants asked to watch the Israelites
   D. Magicians told to curse the Israelites

WEEK 1 MEMORY VERSE: EXODUS 3:14

And God said to Moses, "I AM WHO I AM." And He said, "Thus you shall say to the children of Israel, 'I AM has sent me to you.

WEEK 1

3. Why did Shiphrah and Puah refuse to follow Pharaoh's command? (Exodus 1:17)

A. They were afraid of Moses
B. They feared God and chose to save the babies
C. They didn't understand the king's orders
D. They wanted to please the Israelite mothers

4. How did God bless the midwives for their obedience? (Exodus 1:21)

A. He gave them gold
B. He gave them their own families
C. He made them famous in Egypt
D. He gave them more servants

WEEK 1 MEMORY VERSE: EXODUS 3:14

And God said to Moses, "I AM WHO I AM." And He said, "Thus you shall say to the children of Israel, 'I AM has sent me to you.

WEEK 1

5. How long did Moses' mother hide him before placing him in the Nile? (Exodus 2:1-4)

A. 6 months
B. 3 months
C. 12 months
D. Until he started crying

6. Who found baby Moses floating in the river? (Exodus 2:5-6)

A. Pharaoh's daughter
B. An Egyptian servant
C. Moses' sister
D. A Hebrew woman

WEEK 1 MEMORY VERSE: EXODUS 3:14

And God said to Moses, "I AM WHO I AM." And He said, "Thus you shall say to the children of Israel, 'I AM has sent me to you.

WEEK 1

7. What happened after Moses was found on river Nile? (Exodus 2:6-10)

A. He was returned to his mother to nurse him, then raised by Pharaoh's daughter.
B. He became a soldier in Egypt
C. He was sent to the desert
D. He lived in the palace from birth

8. Why did Moses flee Egypt and go to Midian? (Exodus 2:11-15)

A. He didn't want to live in the palace anymore
B. He was sent away by Pharaoh
C. He had killed an Egyptian and Pharaoh found out
D. He wanted to visit his father-in-law

WEEK 1 MEMORY VERSE: EXODUS 3:14

And God said to Moses, "I AM WHO I AM." And He said, "Thus you shall say to the children of Israel, 'I AM has sent me to you.

"

9. How did the angel of the Lord appear to Moses at Mount Horeb? (Exodus 3: 1-3)

A. As a bright cloud over the mountain
B. In flames of fire within a bush that didn't burn up
C. With golden wings and shining light
D. In a dream while Moses was sleeping

"

10. What did God tell Moses when he approached the burning bush? (Exodus 3:5)

A. "Come closer and see this sign."
B. "Take off your sandals, for this is holy ground."
C. "Do not run away from Me."
D. "Lift up your staff in My name."

WEEK 1 MEMORY VERSE: EXODUS 3:14

And God said to Moses, "I AM WHO I AM." And He said, "Thus you shall say to the children of Israel, 'I AM has sent me to you.

WEEK 1

11. Why did God send Moses back to Egypt? (Exodus 3:10)

A. To apologize to Pharaoh
B. To bring the Israelites out of slavery
C. To protect the Egyptians
D. To live with his family

12. What name did God reveal to Moses at the burning bush? (Exodus 3:13-14)

A. El Shaddai
B. Jehovah Jireh
C. I AM WHO I AM
D. The Most High

WEEK 1 MEMORY VERSE: EXODUS 3:14

And God said to Moses, "I AM WHO I AM." And He said, "Thus you shall say to the children of Israel, 'I AM has sent me to you.

13. What happened when Moses threw his staff on the ground? (Exodus 4:3-4)

A. It burst into flames
B. It turned into a snake
C. It disappeared into the sand
D. It turned into a tree

14. What happened to Moses' hand when he put it inside his cloak (robe)? (Exodus 4:6-7)

A. It froze
B. It became white with leprosy
C. It glowed with God's glory
D. It began to tremble

WEEK 1 MEMORY VERSE: EXODUS 3:14

And God said to Moses, "I AM WHO I AM." And He said, "Thus you shall say to the children of Israel, 'I AM has sent me to you.

KEEP GOING, YOU'RE DOING GREAT!

I belong to the great I AM. Nothing is too hard for Him! (Jeremiah 32:27)

Great job completing the week!

Did you memorize the daily verse?
Test yourself by writing it here...

_____

_____

_____

_____

_____

_____

Use this space to draw a scene from the Bible or reflect
on something you learned, felt or experienced...

"

15. Why did Moses hesitate to go back to Egypt? (Exodus 4:10-13)

A. He feared being punished
B. He had trouble speaking (speech impediment)
C. He wanted to stay in Midian
D. He didn't believe God was real

"

16. What did God tell Pharaoh through Moses and Aaron? (Exodus 5:1)

A. "Let My people go so they may worship Me in the wilderness."
B. "Let My people go or Egypt will fall."
C. "Let My people go to find new land."
D. "Let My people go and make a golden calf."

WEEK 2 MEMORY VERSE: EXODUS 14:14
The LORD himself will fight for you. Just stay calm.

"

17. Why did Pharaoh refuse to let the Israelites go? ((Exodus 5:4-5)

A. He needed their hard labor
B. He didn't believe in God
C. He liked having guests from Israel
D. He was afraid they would take over Egypt

"

18. What did Pharaoh do after Moses and Aaron asked to free the people? (Exodus 5:1-10)

A. He gave the Israelites more work
B. He refused Moses' & Aaron's request
C. He punished the Israelites
D. All the above

WEEK 2 MEMORY VERSE: EXODUS 14:14
The LORD himself will fight for you. Just stay calm.

WEEK 2 »»»»

19. What name of God did He use with Abraham, Isaac, and Jacob? (Exodus 6:3)

A. Lord
B. Jesus
C. King
D. El Shaddai

20. What promises did God make to deliver Israel? (Exodus 6:6)

A. I will bring you out
B. I will deliver you
C. I will redeem you
D. All the above

WEEK 2 MEMORY VERSE: EXODUS 14:14
The LORD himself will fight for you. Just stay calm.

‹‹‹‹‹ WEEK 2 ›››››

21. What happened when Pharaoh's magicians threw down their staffs? (Exodus 7:10-12)

A. Their staffs turned into snakes, but Aaron's staff swallowed them
B. Their staffs turned into frogs
C. Their staffs disappeared
D. Aaron's staff ran away

22. What happened when Aaron struck the Nile River with his staff? (Exodus 7:20-21)

A. The river turned into blood
B. The river split in two
C. The water dried up
D. Nothing happened

WEEK 2 MEMORY VERSE: EXODUS 14:14
The LORD himself will fight for you. Just stay calm.

WEEK 2

23. **What was the second plague sent to Egypt? (Exodus 8:6)**

A. Frogs filled the land
B. Gnats filled the air
C. The river turned to blood
D. Hail destroyed the crops

24. **Which miracle could Pharaoh's magicians NOT copy? (Exodus 8:18)**

A. Turning staffs into snakes
B. Turning water into blood
C. Making frogs appear
D. Creating gnats from dust

WEEK 2 MEMORY VERSE: EXODUS 14:14
The LORD himself will fight for you. Just stay calm.

25. What was different about the land of Goshen during the plague of flies? (Exodus 8:22)

A. It had more flies than the rest of Egypt
B. There were no flies in Goshen
C. The water turned into honey
D. All the livestock died

26. What happened during the fifth plague? (Exodus 9:4-6)

A. All the Egyptian livestock died, but none in Goshen were harmed
B. The livestock in both Egypt and Goshen died
C. The magicians of Egypt became sick
D. Hailstones fell and crushed the cattle

WEEK 2 MEMORY VERSE: EXODUS 14:14
The LORD himself will fight for you. Just stay calm.

WEEK 2

27. Which of these was one of the plagues God sent to Egypt? (Exodus 9 and 10)

A. Hurricanes and tornadoes
B. Locusts, boils, hail, and darkness
C. Malaria, COVID, and the flu
D. The plagues of Moses, Pharaoh, and Aaron

28. What was the final plague that made Pharaoh let the Israelites go? (Exodus 11:4-8)

A. Three days of total darkness
B. The Nile dried up
C. Death of every firstborn child and animal in Egypt
D. The sky turned red for seven days

WEEK 2 MEMORY VERSE: EXODUS 14:14
The LORD himself will fight for you. Just stay calm.

God goes before me, and He fights my battles! (Exodus 14:14)

Great job completing the week!

Did you memorize the daily verse?
Test yourself by writing it here...

_____

_____

_____

_____

_____

Use this space to draw a scene from the Bible or reflect on something you learned, felt or experienced...

29. How did the angel know which houses to "pass over"? (Exodus 12:21-23)

A. The houses had a lamb sleeping by the door
B. The doors had lights turned on
C. The doors were marked with lamb's blood
D. The families were praying outside

30. What is the Feast of Unleavened Bread meant to remind the Israelites of? (Exodus 12:17, 26-27)

A. That they had to eat bread without butter
B. That God spared their homes during the final plague
C. That Pharaoh's heart was soft like bread
D. That they were on a low-carb diet in the wilderness

WEEK 3 MEMORY VERSE: EXODUS 34:6
And the Lord passed before him and proclaimed, "The Lord, the Lord God, merciful and gracious, longsuffering, and abounding in goodness and truth.

31. What did Pharaoh do after the Israelites left Egypt? (Exodus 14:5-9)

A. Sent gifts after them
B. Sent his army to chase them
C. Prayed for them to have a safe journey
D. Closed the borders and locked the gates

32. How did the Israelites cross the Red Sea? (Exodus 14:16, 29)

A. Moses raised his staff and God parted the waters
B. They built boats and paddled across
C. The wind blew them across
D. The sea froze and they walked on ice

WEEK 3 MEMORY VERSE: EXODUS 34:6

And the Lord passed before him and proclaimed, "The Lord, the Lord God, merciful and gracious, longsuffering, and abounding in goodness and truth.

<<<<< WEEK 3 >>>>>

33. What happened to Pharaoh's army at the Red Sea? (Exodus 14:26-28)

A. They crossed safely after Israel
B. They got lost in the fog
C. They were drowned at the Red Sea
D. They built a bridge

34. When the water in the desert was bitter, what did God tell Moses to do? (Exodus 15:23-25)

A. Speak to the water
B. Strike the water with his staff
C. Throw a piece of wood into the water
D. Pour oil into the water

WEEK 3 MEMORY VERSE: EXODUS 34:6
And the Lord passed before him and proclaimed, "The Lord, the Lord God, merciful and gracious, longsuffering, and abounding in goodness and truth.

35. How did God feed the Israelites in the desert? (Exodus 16:4)

A. He caused trees to grow overnight
B. He sent birds every morning
C. He rained down bread from heaven
D. He made fish rise from the sand

36. What did Manna taste like? (Exodus 16:31)

A. Like garlic bread
B. Like wafers made with honey
C. Like roasted lamb
D. Like sweet potatoes

WEEK 3 MEMORY VERSE: EXODUS 34:6

And the Lord passed before him and proclaimed, "The Lord, the Lord God, merciful and gracious, longsuffering, and abounding in goodness and truth.

37. How did God provide water at Rephidim? (Exodus 17:1-6)

A. A river formed in the desert

B. Moses struck a rock with his staff and water gushed out

C. A well suddenly appeared

D. The dew turned into water

38. What did Moses have to do for Israel to win the battle with the Amalekites? (Exodus 17:10-11)

A. Raise his hands and keep them up

B. Blow the trumpet of war

C. Stand on a rock and shout

D. Hold the Ark of the Covenant

WEEK 3 MEMORY VERSE: EXODUS 34:6

And the Lord passed before him and proclaimed, "The Lord, the Lord God, merciful and gracious, longsuffering, and abounding in goodness and truth.

39. How did Aaron and Hur help Moses during the battle between Israel and the Amalekites? (Exodus 17:12)

A. They stood beside him and helped him keep his hands raised
B. They joined the army and fought
C. They built an altar of victory
D. They fetched water for Moses

40. Who was Jethro? (Exodus 18:1-2)

A. Moses' older brother
B. A Midianite priest and Moses' father-in-law
C. An Egyptian soldier
D. The builder of the Ark

WEEK 3 MEMORY VERSE: EXODUS 34:6

And the Lord passed before him and proclaimed, "The Lord, the Lord God, merciful and gracious, longsuffering, and abounding in goodness and truth.

41. How many commandments did God give Israel? (Exodus 20:3-17)

A. 5
B. 10
C. 20
D. 100

42. Which of these is NOT one of the Ten Commandments? (Exodus 20:3-17)

A. You shall not misuse the name of the Lord
B. You shall not covet your neighbor's things
C. You shall have no other gods before Me
D. You shall not pray without kneeling

WEEK 3 MEMORY VERSE: EXODUS 34:6
And the Lord passed before him and proclaimed, "The Lord, the Lord God, merciful and gracious, longsuffering, and abounding in goodness and truth.

God's presence gives me rest!
(Exodus 33:14)

Great job completing the week!

Did you memorize the daily verse?
Test yourself by writing it here...

_____

_____

_____

_____

_____

_____

Use this space to draw a scene from the Bible or reflect
on something you learned, felt or experienced...

WEEK 4

<<<<< **WEEK 4** >>>>>

> **43. What did God command about the Sabbath?**
> **(Exodus 20:8-11)**
>
> A. Work double on the Sabbath to rest later
> B. Rest, just as God did after creation
> C. Fast for 12 hours and wear sackcloth
> D. Only priests were allowed to rest

> **44. What command did God give about honoring**
> **parents? (Exodus 20:12)**
>
> A. Obey them only when they're kind
> B. Honor your father and mother to live long
> C. Only honor them until age 18
> D. Ignore them if they don't agree with you

WEEK 4 MEMORY VERSE: EXODUS 15:2

The Lord is my strength and song, And He has become my salvation; He is my God, and I will praise Him; My father's God, and I will exalt Him.

WEEK 4

<<<<< WEEK 4 >>>>>

45. Which of the following is NOT one of the ten Commandments? (Exodus 20:13-17)

A. Do not steal
B. Do not lie
C. You may give false testimony against your neighbor
D. Do not covet

46. What does Exodus 23:2 say about following the crowd? (Exodus 23:2)

A. Join the crowd and blend in
B. Always stand alone
C. Do not follow the crowd in doing wrong
D. The crowd always knows best

WEEK 4 MEMORY VERSE: EXODUS 15:2
The Lord is my strength and song, And He has become my salvation; He is my God,
and I will praise Him; My father's God, and I will exalt Him.

WEEK 4

47. **What does God say about accepting bribes?**
(Exodus 23:8)

A. Bribes can be given if it's a small amount
B. Never accept a bribe — it blinds and corrupts
C. Bribes are okay if used for church
D. Bribes are part of life

48. **Where did God write the Ten Commandments?**
(Exodus 31:18)

A. On the temple wall
B. In the sky with fire
C. On two stone tablets
D. In the sand

WEEK 4 MEMORY VERSE: EXODUS 15:2

The Lord is my strength and song, And He has become my salvation; He is my God, and I will praise Him; My father's God, and I will exalt Him.

49. What did the Israelites do when Moses took too long on the mountain? (Exodus 32:1-4)

A. Went to search for him

B. Built a golden calf to worship

C. Prayed until he returned

D. Left to find a new leader

50. What did Moses do when he saw the people worshiping the idol? (Exodus 32:19-20)

A. He threw the tablets down and broke them

B. He burned the idol and ground it into powder

C. He scattered the powder in water and made the people drink

D. All the above

WEEK 4 MEMORY VERSE: EXODUS 15:2

The Lord is my strength and song, And He has become my salvation; He is my God, and I will praise Him; My father's God, and I will exalt Him.

WEEK 4

<<<<< **WEEK 4** >>>>>

51. How did God describe the land of Canaan? (Exodus 33:3)

A. A land full of silver and gold

B. A land flowing with milk and honey

C. A land filled with mighty warriors

D. A land covered in palm trees

52. How did God speak to Moses inside the Tent of Meeting? (Exodus 33:11)

A. Through a thunderstorm

B. In a dream

C. Face to face, as one speaks to a friend

D. Through a pillar of fire

WEEK 4 MEMORY VERSE: EXODUS 15:2

The Lord is my strength and song, And He has become my salvation; He is my God, and I will praise Him; My father's God, and I will exalt Him.

"

53. What is the name of Moses' young assistant? (Exodus 33:11)

A. Samuel

B. David

C. Joshua

D. Levi

"

54 . What was different about Moses' face after speaking with God? (Exodus 34:29)

A. His eyes glowed like fire

B. His hair turned white

C. His face was shining with God's glory

D. He was floating slightly above the ground

WEEK 4 MEMORY VERSE: EXODUS 15:2

The Lord is my strength and song, And He has become my salvation; He is my God, and I will praise Him; My father's God, and I will exalt Him.

55. Why did God tell Moses to anoint the Tabernacle and everything in it? (Exodus 40:9)

A. To make them sparkle and shine
B. To set them apart as holy
C. To keep insects away
D. To make the room smell nice

56. Why did God choose Joshua to lead the people across the Jordan River? (Joshua 1:1-2)

A. Because Moses had died, and God chose Joshua to lead His people
B. Because Joshua could swim better than everyone else
C. Because Joshua was young and energetic
D. Because Moses passed him the staff

WEEK 4 MEMORY VERSE: EXODUS 15:2

The Lord is my strength and song, And He has become my salvation; He is my God, and I will praise Him; My father's God, and I will exalt Him.

The Lord is my strength and my song; He is my victory!
(Exodus 15:2)

Great job completing the week!

Did you memorize the daily verse?
Test yourself by writing it here...

_____

_____

_____

_____

_____

_____

Use this space to draw a scene from the Bible or reflect on something you learned, felt or experienced...

INTRODUCTION: THE BOOK OF JOSHUA

Be Strong and Courageous

The Book of Joshua is all about **trusting God and stepping into His promises** with boldness! After Moses died, God chose **Joshua** to lead the Israelites into the land He had promised them.

It wasn't always easy! There were big walls, battles to fight, and instructions that didn't always make sense — but God kept saying:
"Be strong and courageous. I am with you!"

In Joshua, you will see how God helps His people win battles, cross rivers, and conquer giants. But more than that, you will learn how to **listen to God, obey His Word,** and **never give up,** even when it looks impossible.

This book reminds us:
- **God always keeps His promises**
- **Obedience brings blessing**
- **God is our strength and our victory**
- **With God, no battle is too big**

So get ready to cross over, stand firm, and see the walls fall — because with God on your side, you are unstoppable!

"Have I not commanded you? Be strong and of good courage... for the Lord your God is with you wherever you go." — Joshua 1:9

57. What promise did God give to Joshua at the beginning of his leadership? (Joshua 1:5-6)

A. That angels would walk beside him

B. That Moses would return and help

C. That no one would stand against him and God would be with him

D. That he would become king over Israel

58. What command did God give Joshua about the Book of the Law? (the Word of God)? (Joshua 1:7-8)

A. Carry it in a golden box

B. Read it every Sunday

C. Obey and meditate on it day and night

D. Burn it and start a new scroll

WEEK 5 MEMORY VERSE: JOSHUA 1:8

This Book of the Law shall not depart from your mouth, but you shall meditate in it day and night, that you may observe to do according to all that is written in it. For then you will make your way prosperous, and then you will have good success.

59. How many spies did Joshua send to explore Jericho? (Joshua 2:1)

A. Two
B. Four
C. Six
D. Ten

60. How did Rahab help the two Israelite spies? (Joshua 2:4-6)

A. She gave them armor and swords
B. She hid them on the roof of her house
C. She gave them directions to escape
D. She distracted the guards with a dance

WEEK 5 MEMORY VERSE: JOSHUA 1:8

This Book of the Law shall not depart from your mouth, but you shall meditate in it day and night, that you may observe to do according to all that is written in it. For then you will make your way prosperous, and then you will have good success.

61. How did the spies tell Rahab to mark her house for safety? (Joshua 2:17-18)

A. By tying a scarlet cord in her window

B. By waving a white flag

C. By putting a torch outside the door

D. By standing outside with her family

62. What happened to the Jordan River when the priests stepped in with the Ark? (Joshua 3:15-16)

A. It turned into wine

B. The water froze

C. The water stopped flowing and piled up in a heap

D. A bridge formed over the water

WEEK 5 MEMORY VERSE: JOSHUA 1:8

This Book of the Law shall not depart from your mouth, but you shall meditate in it day and night, that you may observe to do according to all that is written in it. For then you will make your way prosperous, and then you will have good success.

63. Where did the priests stand while the people crossed the Jordan? (Joshua 3:17)

A. On the riverbank
B. In the middle of the river
C. At the top of a hill
D. At the edge of the Promised Land

64. Why did the Israelites collect 12 stones from the Jordan River? (Joshua 4:2-7)

A. To build weapons for battle
B. To sell them as souvenirs
C. The stones were to serve as a memorial (reminder) about how God dried up the River for them to cross
D. To stop the river from flowing

WEEK 5 MEMORY VERSE: JOSHUA 1:8
This Book of the Law shall not depart from your mouth, but you shall meditate in it day and night, that you may observe to do according to all that is written in it. For then you will make your way prosperous, and then you will have good success.

65. Why did God dry up the Jordan River for the people of Israel? (Joshua 4:24)

A. So they could go swimming
B. So they could build a bridge
C. So all the nations would know His power and fear the Lord
D. So the priests could wash the Ark

66. What did the angel tell Joshua when he appeared with a drawn sword? (Joshua 5:13-15)

A. "I'm here to destroy Jericho"
B. "The place where you're standing is holy — take off your sandals"
C. "Build a fire and offer a sacrifice"
D. "Get ready to fight me"

WEEK 5 MEMORY VERSE: JOSHUA 1:8

This Book of the Law shall not depart from your mouth, but you shall meditate in it day and night, that you may observe to do according to all that is written in it. For then you will make your way prosperous, and then you will have good success.

67. What strategy did God give Joshua to defeat Jericho? (Joshua 6:2-5)

A. Surround the city and attack at night
B. March around the city for seven days and shout on the seventh day
C. Use flaming arrows and battering rams
D. Dig under the city walls

68. What happened when the Israelites shouted after marching around Jericho? (Joshua 6:20)

A. The walls of Jericho collapsed
B. Lightning struck the city
C. The people of Jericho fled
D. The city gates flew open

WEEK 5 MEMORY VERSE: JOSHUA 1:8

This Book of the Law shall not depart from your mouth, but you shall meditate in it day and night, that you may observe to do according to all that is written in it. For then you will make your way prosperous, and then you will have good success.

69. What warning did Joshua give about rebuilding Jericho? (Joshua 6:26)

A. Anyone who rebuilds it will lose their firstborn and youngest sons
B. God would bless the one who rebuilt it
C. The new city would fall again
D. It must be renamed New Jericho

70. What happened to Rahab and her family during the battle of Jericho? (Joshua 6:23)

A. They escaped before the battle began
B. They were left behind in the city
C. They were rescued and taken to safety
D. They were accidentally harmed

WEEK 5 MEMORY VERSE: JOSHUA 1:8

This Book of the Law shall not depart from your mouth, but you shall meditate in it day and night, that you may observe to do according to all that is written in it. For then you will make your way prosperous, and then you will have good success.

God's Word is my guide, and I walk in His truth (Psalm 119:105)

Great job completing the week!

Did you memorize the daily verse?
Test yourself by writing it here...

_____

_____

_____

_____

_____

_____

Use this space to draw a scene from the Bible or reflect
on something you learned, felt or experienced...

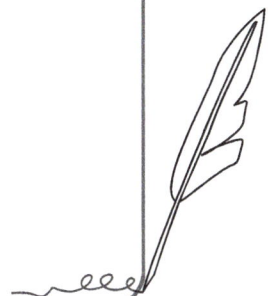

71. What did Achan steal from Jericho that was forbidden? (Joshua 7:20-21)

A. A golden calf and a silver bowl

B. A beautiful robe, silver, and a bar of gold

C. A sword and a pair of sandals

D. A scroll and a crown

72 What instruction did God give Joshua to defeat the city of Ai? (Joshua 8:18-19)

A. March around Ai like Jericho

B. Use horses and chariots

C. Set an ambush and hold out your javelin toward the city

D. Send spies again and pray at the gate

WEEK 6 MEMORY VERSE: JOSHUA 1:9
Have I not commanded you? Be strong and of good courage; do not be afraid,
nor be dismayed, for the Lord your God is with you wherever you go.

WEEK 6

> **73. How did Joshua build the altar to the Lord after the victory? (Joshua 8:30-31)**
>
> A. With smooth stones from the river
> B. Using uncut stones with no tools used on them
> C. With bricks and mortar
> D. With gold from Jericho

> **74. How did Joshua teach the people God's Law? (Joshua 8:32-35)**
>
> A. He wrote it on scrolls and gave everyone a copy
> B. He had the elders read it out loud
> C. He wrote it on stones and read every word to the people
> D. He memorized it and taught them songs

WEEK 6 MEMORY VERSE: JOSHUA 1:9
Have I not commanded you? Be strong and of good courage; do not be afraid, nor be dismayed, for the Lord your God is with you wherever you go.

75. How did the Gibeonites trick Joshua into making a peace treaty? (Joshua 9:1-6)

A. They dressed in royal clothes and claimed to be kings
B. They pretended to be injured and begged for healing
C. They wore old clothes and brought moldy bread, pretending to be from far away
 D. They pretended to be prophets of God

76. What did Joshua do when he found out that the people of Gibeon had lied? (Joshua 9:22–23)

A. He destroyed their city
B. He chased them out of the land
C. He made them servants—woodcutters and water carriers
D. He told them never to return

WEEK 6 MEMORY VERSE: JOSHUA 1:9
Have I not commanded you? Be strong and of good courage; do not be afraid, nor be dismayed, for the Lord your God is with you wherever you go.

WEEK 6

77. Why did the five kings come together to attack the Gibeonites? (Joshua 10:3-4)

A. Because the Gibeonites were strong in battle
B. Because Gibeon had made peace with Israel
C. Because they wanted to conquer Egypt
D. Because they were tired of fighting each other

78. What did Joshua command the sun and the moon to do during battle? (Joshua 10:12)

A. To disappear over the horizon
B. To reflect God's glory
C. To stand still
D. To shine brighter than usual

WEEK 6 MEMORY VERSE: JOSHUA 1:9
Have I not commanded you? Be strong and of good courage; do not be afraid, nor be dismayed, for the Lord your God is with you wherever you go.

WEEK 6

79. How did God help Israel defeat the five Amorite kings? (Joshua 10:10–11)

A. He sent lightning to destroy them

B. He made the ground swallow their horses

C. He confused their enemies and sent hailstones

D. He made their swords burn with fire

80. Why were Joshua and his army so successful in battle? (Joshua 10:42)

A. They had a strong leader

B. They were well trained

C. The Lord fought for them

D. They used clever strategies

WEEK 6 MEMORY VERSE: JOSHUA 1:9
Have I not commanded you? Be strong and of good courage; do not be afraid, nor be dismayed, for the Lord your God is with you wherever you go.

81. What does the Bible say about Joshua's obedience to God? (Joshua 11:15)

A. He did everything the Lord had commanded

B. He obeyed some of God's instructions

C. He left a few enemies unconquered

D. He doubted God's instructions sometimes

82. How many kings did Joshua defeat? (Joshua 12:24)

A. 21

B. 31

C. 40

D. 12

WEEK 6 MEMORY VERSE: JOSHUA 1:9

Have I not commanded you? Be strong and of good courage; do not be afraid, nor be dismayed, for the Lord your God is with you wherever you go.

WEEK 6

83. Of the 12 tribes of Israel, which one did not receive an inheritance?
(Joshua 13:14, Joshua 18:7)

A. Judah

B. Benjamin

C. Levi

D. Dan

84. What inheritance did the Levites receive? (Joshua 14: 1-5)

A. Gold and silver

B. They received no inheritance except cities to live in and grasslands for their animals

C. A portion of each tribe's land

D. Their own section in the wilderness

WEEK 6 MEMORY VERSE: JOSHUA 1:9
Have I not commanded you? Be strong and of good courage; do not be afraid, nor be dismayed, for the Lord your God is with you wherever you go.

" Even when I am afraid, I
will put my trust in God
(Psalm 56:3)

Great job completing the week!

Did you memorize the daily verse?
Test yourself by writing it here...

_____

_____

_____

_____

_____

_____

Use this space to draw a scene from the Bible or reflect on something you learned, felt or experienced...

WEEK 7

85. How old was Caleb when Moses sent him to spy the land? (Joshua 14:7)

A. 30

B. 35

C. 40

D. 45

86. What was the reward given to Caleb for following God wholeheartedly? (Joshua 14:13-14)

A. He was made the King of Israel

B. He was given the land of Hebron as his inheritance

C. He was given many gifts by the people of Israel

D. He was given the land of Shiloh

WEEK 7 MEMORY VERSE: JOSHUA 24:15
But as for me and my house, we will serve the Lord.

WEEK 7

87. What reward did Caleb give to Othniel for conquering Kiriath-sepher? (Joshua 15:15-17)

A. A gold chain

B. He gave him his daughter Aksah in marriage

C. A chariot and horses

D. A field with springs

88. What special favor did Caleb's daughter ask of her father? (Joshua 15:18-19)

A. A feast in her honor

B. Her own tent

C. A field with upper and lower springs

D. A necklace of precious stones

WEEK 7 MEMORY VERSE: JOSHUA 24:15
But as for me and my house, we will serve the Lord.

WEEK 7

89. **What group of people still live with the people of Judah? (Joshua 15:63)**

A . The Perizzites
B. The Jebusites
C. The Hittites
D. The Amorites

90. **What group of people still live with the people of Ephraim? (Joshua 16:10)**

A. The Canaanites
B. The Philistines
C. The Gibeonites
D. The Jebusites

WEEK 7 MEMORY VERSE: JOSHUA 24:15
But as for me and my house, we will serve the Lord.

WEEK 7

91. How did the five daughters of Zelophehad speak up for their inheritance? (Joshua 17:3-6)

A. They went to the Tabernacle and prayed

B. They cried out to the priests

C. They stood before Eleazar the priest and Joshua, and asked for their father's inheritance

D. They asked Moses directly

92. Why did the people of Joseph ask Joshua for additional land? (Joshua 17:14-17)

A. Because the hill country was not enough for them

B. Because they didn't like their inheritance

C. Because their land was dry

D. Because their land was taken by enemies

WEEK 7 MEMORY VERSE: JOSHUA 24:15
But as for me and my house, we will serve the Lord.

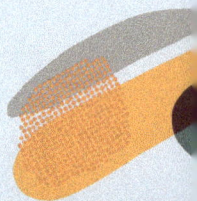

WEEK 7

> 93. **Where did the inheritance for the Simeonites come from? (Joshua 19:9)**

A. From the land of Benjamin
B. From the land of Judah
C. From the land of Reuben
D. From the land of Dan

> 94. **Did Joshua inherit any land?**
> **(Joshua 19:49-50)**

A. No, he was a leader and did not need any
B. Yes, he asked for a specific city and it was given to him
C. Yes, he took the best part of the land by force
D. No, because he was not from the tribe of Judah

WEEK 7 MEMORY VERSE: JOSHUA 24:15
But as for me and my house, we will serve the Lord.

WEEK 7

> ## 95. Why did the Lord ask Joshua to set apart cities of Refuge? (Joshua 20: 1-3, 9)
>
> A. So the Levites would have places to live
> B. To give the people more cities to conquer
> C. So a person who killed someone accidentally could flee there
> D. To store extra supplies for battle

> ## 96. How long was a fugitive to live in the city of refuge? (Joshua 20:6)
>
> A. Until they turned 30
> B. Until the death of the high priest
> C. For seven years
> D. For the rest of their life

WEEK 7 MEMORY VERSE: JOSHUA 24:15
But as for me and my house, we will serve the Lord.

WEEK 7

97. What does the Bible say about God's promises to Israel? (Joshua 21:45)

A. Most of them came true

B. A few of them were forgotten

C. Not one of them failed

D. Only the promises of Moses were fulfilled

98. What are the commands of the law of Moses? (Joshua 22:5)

A. To love the Lord your God and walk in obedience to Him

B. To keep God's commandments and to hold fast to Him

C. To serve God with all your heart and with all your soul

D. All the above

WEEK 7 MEMORY VERSE: JOSHUA 24:15

But as for me and my house, we will serve the Lord.

BONUS QUESTIONS

99. Why did the Reubenites and Gadites build an altar for themselves? (Joshua 22:28, 34)

A. They had rebelled and started worshiping other gods

B. They didn't want to travel far to offer sacrifices

C. They wanted the altar to stand as a witness between them and the rest of Israel that the Lord is God

D. The Lord told them to build an altar on their side of the Jordan

100. What did Joshua say would happen if the people turned away from God and worshiped other gods? (Joshua 23:16)

A. The Lord's anger would burn against them, and they would quickly perish from the good land He had given them

B. They would be attacked by the Canaanites and neighboring nations

C. They would all die in Canaan

D. It would rain for 40 days and nights and flood the land

WEEK 7 MEMORY VERSE: JOSHUA 24:15

But as for me and my house, we will serve the Lord.

BONUS QUESTIONS

101. What did Terah, the father of Abraham and Nahor, do before the Lord took Abraham to Canaan? (Joshua 24:2)

A. He worked as a carpenter

B. He worshiped other gods

C. He was a priest of the Lord

D. He was a farmer

102. What did Joshua say to the people about serving God? (Joshua 24: 14-15)

A. He told them to choose whether they would serve the Lord or the gods their ancestors worshiped

B. He told them that as for him and his household, they would serve the Lord

C. Both A and B

D. None of the above

WEEK 7 MEMORY VERSE: JOSHUA 24:15

But as for me and my house, we will serve the Lord.

BONUS QUESTIONS

103. How old was Joshua when he died?
(Joshua 24:29)

A. 110 years old
B. 85 years old
C. 150 years old
D. 120 years old

104. Where were Joseph's bones buried?
(Joshua 24:32)

A. In Egypt
B. At Shechem, in the land Jacob had bought
C. In the same tomb as Joshua
D. In the valley of Rephaim

WEEK 7 MEMORY VERSE: JOSHUA 24:15
But as for me and my house, we will serve the Lord.

I am set apart for God's special purpose!

(2 Timothy 2:21)

Great job completing the week!

Did you memorize the daily verse?
Test yourself by writing it here...

_____

_____

_____

_____

_____

_____

Use this space to draw a scene from the Bible or reflect
on something you learned, felt or experienced...

Certificate of Completion

This Certificate Certifies That:

_____

Has Successfully Completed The Exodus & Joshua Workbook!

Flo & Grace

_____   _____

PARENT/TEACHER SIGNATURE   **PROJECT KINGDOM COME**

WOULD YOU LIKE TO ACCEPT JESUS INTO YOUR HEART?

THE BIBLE SAYS:

If you confess with your mouth that Jesus is Lord and believe in your heart that God has raised Him from the dead, you will be saved
(Romans 10:9)

SAY THE PRAYER BELOW OUT LOUD AND BELIEVE IT IN YOUR HEART!

Dear Lord Jesus,
I know that I am a sinner, and I ask for Your forgiveness.
I believe You died for my sins and rose from the dead.
I repent of my sins and invite You to come into my heart and life.
I want to trust and follow You as my Lord and Savior. Help me to live for you for the rest of my life.
I am now a child of God, and I ask You to fill me with Your Holy Spirit.

In Jesus' Name I pray, Amen.

Congratulations!

If you have prayed this prayer, please let an adult know or send an email to mybibleworkbooks@gmail.com

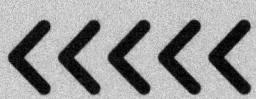 **ANSWER KEY:**

1.B	13.B	25.B
2.B	14.B	26.A
3.B	15.B	27.B
4.B	16.A	28.C
5.B	17.A	29.C
6.A	18.D	30.B
7.A	19.D	31.B
8.C	20.D	32.A
9.B	21.A	33.C
10.B	22.A	34.C
11.B	23.A	35.C
12.C	24.D	36.B

37.B	49.B	61.A
38.A	50.D	62.C
39.A	51.B	63.B
40.B	52.C	64.C
41.B	53.C	65.C
42.D	54.C	66.B
43.B	55.B	67.B
44.B	56.A	68.A
45.C	57.C	69.A
46.C	58.C	70.C
47.B	59.A	71.B
48.C	60.B	72.C

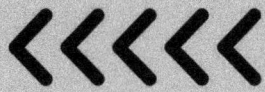 **ANSWER KEY:**

73.B	85.C	
74.C	86.B	
75.C	87.B	97.C
76.C	88.C	98.D
77.B	89.B	99.C
78.C	90.A	100.A
79.C	91.C	101.B
80.C	92.A	102.C
81.A	93.B	103.A
82.B	94.B	104.B
83.C	95.C	
84.B	96.B	

PLEASE GIVE US YOUR FEEDBACK!

Please send us your feedback on this workbook. We would love to hear what you enjoyed most, and ways you think it could be improved!

Please Send an email to: MyBibleWorkbooks@gmail.com, or leave us a comment on one of our social media pages.

✉ MyBibleWorkbooks@gmail.com

📷 Projectkingdomcome

f Projectkingdomcome

SCAN ME

"

And I am certain that God, who began the good work within you, will continue His work until it is finally finished on the day when Christ Jesus returns.

Philippians 1:6

"

DRAW HERE

DRAW HERE

DRAW HERE

DRAW HERE

DRAW HERE

www.ingramcontent.com/pod-product-compliance
Lightning Source LLC
Chambersburg PA
CBHW061409090426
42740CB00026B/3491